S. Hrg. 103–987

NOMINATIONS OF VICE ADM. ROBERT E. KRAMEK TO BE COMMANDANT AND REAR ADM. ARTHUR E. HENN TO BE VICE COMMANDANT OF THE U.S. COAST GUARD

HEARING

BEFORE THE

COMMITTEE ON COMMERCE, SCIENCE, AND TRANSPORTATION UNITED STATES SENATE

ONE HUNDRED THIRD CONGRESS

SECOND SESSION

MAY 3, 1994

Printed for the use of the Committee on Commerce, Science, and Transportation

U.S. GOVERNMENT PRINTING OFFICE

78–790 CC   WASHINGTON : 1995

For sale by the U.S. Government Printing Office
Superintendent of Documents, Congressional Sales Office, Washington, DC 20402

ISBN 0-16-046855-8

(II)

CONTENTS

(III)

NOMINATIONS OF VICE ADM. ROBERT E. KRAMEK TO BE COMMANDANT AND REAR ADM. ARTHUR E. HENN TO BE VICE COMMANDANT OF THE U.S. COAST GUARD

TUESDAY, MAY 3, 1994

U.S. SENATE,
COMMITTEE ON COMMERCE, SCIENCE, AND TRANSPORTATION,
Washington, DC.

The committee met, pursuant to notice, at 10 a.m. in room SR–253, Russell Senate Office Building, Hon. Ernest F. Hollings (chairman of the committee) presiding.

Staff members assigned to this hearing: Rebecca A. Kojm, professional staff member; and Emily J. Gallop, minority professional staff member.

OPENING STATEMENT OF SENATOR HOLLINGS

The CHAIRMAN. The committee will come to order. This morning the Commerce Committee is holding a hearing on the nominations of Vice Adm. Robert E. Kramek to be the Commandant and Rear Adm. Arthur E. Henn to be the Vice Commandant of the U.S. Coast Guard.

These are especially challenging times for the Coast Guard. It continues to be called upon to carry out a number of important missions. From responding to oilspills to participating in military operations, the Coast Guard has been on the front line.

In order for the Coast Guard to continue its tradition of excellence, it must have strong qualified leadership. Admiral Kramek and Admiral Henn provide just this type of leadership.

Rear Admiral Kramek presently is the Chief of Staff of the Coast Guard, serving as commanding officer of the U.S. Coast Guard Headquarters and the senior Rear Admiral. He is both a surface operations specialist and naval engineer with extensive service in all Coast Guard regions, including the Atlantic, Pacific, Caribbean, and Alaska. Admiral Kramek has headed the Haitian Migration Task Force and was the coordinator for the war on drugs in the Southeastern United States and Caribbean.

A native of New York City, he is a 1961 graduate of the Coast Guard Academy. His postgraduate education includes master of science degrees in naval architecture and marine engineering, mechanical engineering, and engineering management. He attended postgraduate school at the University of Michigan, Johns Hopkins University, and the University of Alaska. Admiral Kramek's awards include the Coast Guard Distinguished Service Medal, two

Legion of Merit awards, a Meritorious Service Medal, Coast Guard commendation and achievement medals, and the Humanitarian Service Medal with a Bronze Star.

Rear Admiral Henn currently is the head of the Coast Guard Office of Marine Safety, Security, and Environmental Protection. For 21 of his 31 years of service, he has specialized in maritime safety and environmental protection. A 1962 graduate of the Coast Guard Academy, Admiral Henn also earned combined master of science degrees in naval architecture, marine engineering, and metallurgical engineering from the University of Michigan in 1968. He is a native of Cincinnati, OH. Admiral Henn's awards include the Legion of Merit, two Meritorious Service Medals, Coast Guard commendation and achievement medals, and two Commandant's letters of commendation ribbons.

Before welcoming you to committee, let me yield to our distinguished chairman of the appropriations—I would say for the Coast Guard, it says Defense, but he saves us every year. And, excuse me, I did not see you. You wanted to comment before our distinguished colleague. Oh, you are going to introduce the witnesses. That is fine. Senator Stevens, we welcome you.

OPENING STATEMENT OF SENATOR STEVENS

Senator STEVENS. Well, if you can hear me. I am just out of a dental chair with another root canal, so you can tread easy.

The CHAIRMAN. That is good treatment for you. Speak softly. That is wonderful. I am on the side of that dentist. [Laughter.]

Senator STEVENS. Well, I am here, Mr. Chairman, and my good friend from Hawaii, to introduce the next commandant of the Coast Guard. But, first, I think this is Admiral Kime's last visit to our committee. He has been a great friend and served the Coast Guard well for over 37 years. I hope that we will have the opportunity to recognize this service when he makes his appearance.

But I do come to the committee to introduce Vice Adm. Robert E. Kramek, who will become the 20th Commandant of the Coast Guard. He is currently the Chief of Staff of the Coast Guard, the commanding officer of the Coast Guard Headquarters. He has had a long and distinguished career, beginning in 1961. He graduated with honors from the Coast Guard Academy. He served our country literally in all regions—Atlantic, Pacific, Caribbean, and Alaska. He was commandant of the 13th Coast Guard District in the Pacific Northwest, and of the 7th District in the Southeast United States and the Caribbean. He has also served as commander of the Coast Guard's largest base, Governors Island in New York.

He has advanced degrees in naval architecture and marine engineering, mechanical engineering, and engineering management. Incidentally, while stationed in the 17th district, he obtained his masters of science and engineering management from the University of Alaska. He comes very well educated, Mr. Chairman.

He attended the U.S. Naval War College and received numerous awards for his service and dedication, and from 1972 to 1975 he served as chief of naval engineering in the 17th district in Juneau. From 1981 to 1991 he was the commanding officer of the high-endurance cutter *Midget*, which conducted international fisheries enforcement missions in the North Pacific and the Bering Sea.

Now, I am here primarily because of his experience in our part of the world, but also I want to emphasize how important it is for the Coast Guard to continue the role that they have undertaken. They are not only protecting the lives of our people at sea, but they are also enforcing the laws which protect our vast fishing grounds. The Coast Guard is an absolute integral part of my State, as you know. In Alaska, they serve as everything from midwives to helpers who transport us in times of emergency with their helicopters. I really am delighted to see that the next Commandant of the Coast Guard has such vast experience.

Incidentally, I note that Read Admiral Henn also is here. I am not supposed to introduce him, but I am happy to see that he will be coming on board at this time also. The responsibilities that we have given the Coast Guard, particularly in view of budgetary restraints, means that these gentlemen have a very difficult watch, and I am pleased to have the honor to present them to the committee.

The CHAIRMAN. Well, Senator Stevens, we thank you.

Admiral Kramek, no one has a greater interest in the Coast Guard, no one is a greater protector of the Coast Guard's interest than the Senator from Alaska. And you are honored and the committee is honored to have him present you. We would welcome you and Admiral Henn both, and we would be delighted to hear from you.

STATEMENT OF VICE ADM. ROBERT E. KRAMEK, CHIEF OF STAFF AND COMMANDANT-DESIGNATE, U.S. COAST GUARD

Admiral KRAMEK Good morning, Mr. Chairman. I am pleased to appear before you and the other members of this distinguished committee today, and I particularly thank Senator Stevens for introducing me.

I would like to make a summary of my opening statement and submit the full statement for the record, if I may.

The CHAIRMAN. It will be included in its entirety, and you highlight it as you wish.

Admiral KRAMEK Thank you, Mr. Chairman.

I am deeply honored by the President's nomination to serve as the 20th Commandant of the Coast Guard. I also appreciate the time many Members have taken to meet with me during the last several weeks to discuss Coast Guard priorities during the coming years.

As Senator Stevens mentioned, we are all aware of the excellent job the present Commandant, Admiral Kime, has done in guiding the Coast Guard through the past 4 years. He has provided an excellent base which I will use to build on during my tour as the Commandant. We have planned a seamless transition together.

I sincerely believe that I have the experience, ability, and energy necessary to lead the Coast Guard for the next 4 years, and I look forward to that. As Commandant, I intend to improve the Coast Guard's reputation as the world's premier maritime service, and I will use strong leadership and sound management to encourage all of our Coast Guard personnel to participate in our missions in a very very professional and effective way.

The Coast Guard is an organization that epitomizes excellence and total quality management, and our focus will remain on serving all of our customers at all times. The biggest challenge I face, however, will be streamlining our agency, along with the rest of the Federal Government, while still maintaining service to the public.

This downsizing, while maintaining customer satisfaction, is a challenge for all of us, and I look forward to that. I am going to work closely with Admiral Henn to have the Coast Guard lead in the Department of Transportation and be able to accomplish that. I see a revitalized and expanded research and development program as a key to success in this area because I need to use modern technology to help us work smarter, not just harder.

Achieving diversity is critical to my goal of a quality organization. The Coast Guard cannot be an employer of choice unless we clearly demonstrate that we value the contributions of all Americans. I will work hard to identify and eliminate the cultural barriers we may have in our organization to diversity, and I am committed to making the Coast Guard more representative of our total population, especially promoting women and minorities to top management positions. The Coast Guard's most important asset, as it is for all of us, is our people, and to meet the opportunities and challenges that lie ahead they must be properly trained, equipped, and supported, and that will be my major priority.

Together with other modes in the Department of Transportation, I will support the Secretary in his efforts of intermodalism and lead the Coast Guard in developing a more efficient, effective, and safe waterways transportation system. We will maintain our leadership in marine environmental protection, we will maintain our leadership and traditional role in maritime safety, and we will have a balanced law enforcement program.

We have to work closely with the National Marine Fisheries Service to meet the needs of our Nation's fishing industry and to protect our fisherman. As we are well aware, many of our fishing stocks are depleted. Great grounds in the North Atlantic have been closed down, the great salmon grounds off the coast of Washington have been closed down, and we have some dire circumstances out there in our Exclusive Economic Zone.

However, enforcement of U.S. law regarding illegal migrants, which is big business for the Coast Guard every day, will continue to be a high priority for me, as well as continuing the Coast Guard's leadership role in maritime drug interdiction. And on June 1, I have been informed, when I relieve Admiral Kime, I will also be designated as the U.S. Interdiction Coordinator for the interdiction of drugs in the Western Hemisphere. I will report, as a separate duty, to Dr. Lee Brown, the head of the Office of National Drug Control Policy, and be responsible to the President for the interdiction portion of his national drug strategy.

The Coast Guard will continue to meet its national security responsibilities and be a valued member of the Armed Forces, participating in joint exercises, helping our sister services when we can and where we can. I have met with all of the top members of the other Services, including General Shalikashvili last week, to talk about our participation with the other members of the Armed Forces.

I will work with the administration and Congress to ensure the Coast Guard is responsive to all the national priorities that are set forward to me, and make sure that the Coast Guard has the necessary resources to do the job.

Thank you very much for the opportunity to appear before you today, and I will be happy to respond to any questions that you may have.

Senator INOUYE. Admiral Kramek, on behalf of the committee I thank you for your statement. Before proceeding, the chairman of the committee, Senator Hollings, submitted to you a list of questions and so if I may, without objection, the questions and your responses will be made part of the record.

Admiral KRAMEK Yes, sir, I will submit them for the record.

[The prepared statement and prehearing questions and answers of Admiral Kramek follow:]

PREPARED STATEMENT OF VICE ADM. ROBERT E. KRAMEK

Good morning, Mr. Chairman. I am pleased to appear before you and the other members of this distinguished committee today.

I am deeply honored by the President's nomination to serve as the twentieth Commandant of the United States Coast Guard. I also appreciate the time many of you have taken to meet with me to discuss Coast Guard priorities for the coming years.

In my thirty-three years of service, I have found the Coast Guard to be a highly competent and professional organization. These attributes, coupled with our dedicated people, our military organization and discipline, our command and control structure, our support structure, and our inventory of highly capable multi-mission resources, give us unmatched flexibility and responsiveness. In my opinion the Coast Guard is the most efficient and effective organization in the Federal Government.

You are aware of the excellent job the present Commandant, Admiral J. William Kime, has done in guiding the Coast Guard through the past four years. He has provided an excellent base on which I hope to build during my tour as Commandant.

I sincerely believe that I have the experience, ability and energy necessary to lead the Coast Guard for the next four years. As Commandant, I will improve the Coast Guard's reputation as the world's premier maritime service. I will use our strong leadership and sound management to guide and encourage all Coast Guard people— regular, reserve, officer, enlisted, civilian, auxiliary—to achieve an even higher level of public service excellence. Certainly, this administration and Congress have created an environment that provides unprecedented opportunities for accomplishment. I look forward to working with the President, Secretary Peña, and the Congress to meet this goal. Also, I am very pleased with Rear Admiral Henn's nomination to be my Vice Commandant. He will serve with distinction.

The Coast Guard has proudly served our nation for 204 years, and I see us as being well positioned to enter the next century. I pledge that we will continue to provide the highest possible quality of service to the American public and the world in our four major mission areas; maritime safety, protection of the marine environment, maritime law enforcement, and national security.

I envision the Coast Guard as an organization that epitomizes quality management. We will focus on serving our customers at all times. We will gain recognition as the employer of choice for a diverse work force, which streamlines along with the rest of the federal government, while maintaining essential customer services, especially those that relate to safety.

I see quality management as the key to our ability to continue to deliver essential services to our customers. As I stated earlier, I believe the Coast Guard is already a lean and effective organization * * * my challenge is to make it even more efficient and more effective. I see a revitalized and expanded research and development program as a key to success in this area. We need modern technology to help us work smarter * * * not just harder.

Achieving diversity is critical to my goal of a quality organization. The Coast Guard can not be the employer of choice unless we clearly demonstrate that we value the contributions of all Americans. I will work hard to identify and eliminate cultural barriers to diversity * * * I am committed to making the Coast Guard more representative of our nation's total population and promoting women and minorities to top management positions.

Success requires team work. As my predecessors have always done, I will look to the Coast Guard's most important asset, its people, to meet the opportunities and challenges that lie ahead. If we are to succeed they must be properly trained, equipped, and supported. Accordingly, programs that ensure proper training and adequate medical care, housing, and compensation will be one of my highest priorities.

As chief of staff, I have already established strong partnerships in the Department of Transportation, which will help the Coast Guard contribute to the development of a more efficient, effective, safe, and customer oriented transportation network. I envision an improved national waterway and port management infrastructure that is integrated with other transportation systems. This is needed to facilitate the expansion of international trade, which will be an increasingly important element of our national economy.

The Coast Guard will continue to maintain its national and international leadership position in marine environmental protection. The improved, modern port and waterway system I just spoke of is a key to maintaining clean waterways, but we also need to continue our work to identify and aggressively prosecute national and international polluters.

Our traditional maritime safety mission will continue as a national priority. I will further our role as "lifesavers" represented by the search and rescue, aids to navigation, and commercial vessel safety programs. I intend to sharpen our focus on prevention, while remaining always ready to respond to those in distress.

A balanced law enforcement program will remain a major Coast Guard mission. I look forward to continuing a close relationship with the National Marine Fisheries Service as we work together to meet the needs of our nation's fishing industry and restore our nation's fisheries stocks. Enforcement of U.S. law regarding illegal migrants will continue as a high priority Coast Guard mission. And, I am committed to continuing the Coast Guard's leadership role in maritime drug interdiction.

The Coast Guard will continue to meet its national security responsibilities. I will work to properly align our military capabilities with the realities and threats of an evolving national security environment. We will remain a valued member of the nation's Armed Forces, participate in joint exercises, respond to national security emergencies when needed.

I will work with the administration and the Congress to ensure the Coast Guard is responsive to national priorities, and has the necessary resources to provide the highest possible quality of service to the American public. I will ensure those resources are used as efficiently and effectively as possible.

Thank you for the opportunity to appear before you today. I will be happy to respond to any questions you might have.

QUESTIONS ASKED BY SENATOR HOLLINGS AND ANSWERS THERETO BY ADMIRAL KRAMEK

PRIORITIES AND CHALLENGES

Question. After more than three decades of Coast Guard service, you have had a broad exposure to the agency's missions and the opportunity to observe Coast Guard operations in virtually every part of the country. Given your diverse experience, what are your immediate and long-range priorities for the Coast guard. If confirmed, what do you see as the most important challenges facing you as Commandant?

Answer. The Coast Ouard is the world's leading maritime service. The primary long-term challenge we face is to maintain essential services to our customers as we concurrently engage with the rest of the Executive Branch in streamlining efforts. You have my assurance that public safety will not be compromised. With your help, I am confident in our ability to meet this challenge. It will require good program management, maintenance of strong support systems and. most of all, continued ability to attract highly qualified people.

As Chief of Staff, I established strong partnership ties with the Department so that Coast Guard can contribute to Secretary Peña's goal of developing a better transportation network. I envision an improved National Waterway and Port Management infrastructure that is integrated with other transportation systems. This is needed to facilitate the expansion of international trade, which will be an ncreasingly important element of our national economy.

The Coast Guard will continue to maintain its national and international leadership position in Marine Environmental Protection. The improved, modern port and waterway system mentioned above is a key to maintaining clean waterways, but we also need to continue our work to identify and aggressively prosecute national and international polluters.

Our traditional Maritime Safety mission will continue as a national priority. I will further our safety role as "lifesavers" through the Search and Rescue, Aids to Navigation, and Commercial Vessel Safety Programs. The increased focus here will be prevention, while remaining always ready to respond to those in distress.

A balanced Law Enforcement program will remain a major Coast Guard mission. I look forward to continuing a close relationship with the national Marine Fisheries Service as we work together to meet the needs of our nation's fishing industry and restore our nation's fisheries stocks. Enforcement of U.S. laws regarding illegal migrants will continue as a high priority Coast Guard mission. I am committed to continuing the Coast Guard's leadership role in Maritime Drug Interdiction.

The Coast Guard will continue to meet its National Security responsibilities. I will work to properly align our military capabilities with the realities and threats of an evolving National security environment. We will remain a valued member of the Nation's Armed Forces, participate in joint exercises, and respond to National security emergencies when needed.

One of my priorities will be to continue to seek adequate resources to recapitalize Coast Guard operating assets, replacing old obsolete, high maintenance equipment with modern, efficient, hardware. Pressures on our operating expense budget demand that we drive toward a more efficient capital plant. Pressures on our Operating Expenses Appropriation demand that we drive toward a more efficient capital plant. I will emphasize a systems approach to acquisition to ensure efficiency through integration.

Part of this approach is a revitalized and expanded Research and Technology Program as a key to success. We need modern technology to help us work smarter, not just harder.

And we will continue to attend to the most important resource of all—our people. I am committed to making the Coast Guard more representative of our nation's total population and promoting women and minorities to top management positions. Our changing demographic environment requires this for the Coast Guard to continue as an employer of choice for some of the best and brightest in our nation. To attract the best, we will eliminate any cultural barriers to diversity. By our own example, we will foster in them the values of honor, respect, and devotion to service. We will retain them by providing the training, equipment, and other support which allows them to do the best possible job.

I will work with the Administration and the Congress to ensure the Coast Guard is responsive to national priorities, and has the necessary resources to provide the highest possible quality of service to the American public. I will ensure those resources are used as efficiently and effectively as possible.

CAPITAL ASSET BUDGET SITUATION

Question. The Coast Guard currently maintains capital assets worth almost $17 billion, including ships, aircraft, and shoreside facilities. By the agency's own estimates, about $600 million is needed annually to maintain this infrastructure. However, the annual budget request and funding for acquisitions and improvements usually falls far short of the level, and the Administration's request for $439 million in fiscal year 1995 is no exception. If confirmed, how do you propose to deal with this budget situation?

Answer. You will hear later this morning from Admiral Kime that adequate funding for replacement and improvement of Coast Guard capital assets is one of our highest priorities for this year's budget. As the Chief of Staff, I've worked closely with the Commandant on this budget issue to ensure the continued availability of sufficient capital resources for conducting Coast Guard missions. If confirmed as the next Commandant, I will continue the initiatives that we have put in place to determine and justify an adequate capital account budget.

$439 million is sufficient funding for FY 1995, but we will soon begin consuming our capital plant if our mission requirements remain the same, or continue to grow, and we don't increase our rate of capitalization. The $600 million figure that you reference is a theoretical replacement rate computed from the current value of our capital assets and their expected service life. It's a planning figure for a one-for-one type replacement scheme that I realize will be difficult to achieve in the current budget climate. However, this theoretical value has proven to be a reliable indicator of capital requirements because we need over $500 million a year for the rest of this decade just to complete the current approved major system acquisitions that you see in our budget, while maintaining a minimum level of funding for overhauls, improvements and shore construction projects. In fact, capital investments in the range of $500-600 million during the rest of this decade are necessary if we are to effectively use technology and modern equipment and facilities to help us attain the efficiencies in operating expenses demanded by existing budget caps.

As the next Commandant, I would continue to work with OST and OMB to link our capital budget to our operational requirements and the need to drive down total lifecycle costs of our operational assets. which include operations and maintenance expenses as well as acquisition costs. I would look at future requirements in a systems approach, similar to our efforts in the buoy tender replacement acquisition where we looked at the entire fleet as a system and then applied the latest technology in the replacement vessels. The result will be fewer ships with smaller crews providing increased service to the public because of the additional oil spill recovery capabilities of the seagoing buoy tender. Total fleet operating costs will be reduced by almost $25 million a year. but we must make a timely committed investment of AC&I dollars to realize these savings.

Mission analysis. multi-year budget strategies. capital investment plans and exploitation of technology are the keys to determining operational requirements and the least costly alternative in meeting them. If confirmed as the next Commandant, I would continue the emphasis that we have begun in these areas and build capital budgets that assure you, the Administration and the taxpayer that we are making the wisest investment of capital funds to maintain essential services to the public.

ALIEN MIGRATION INTERDICTION OPERATIONS

Question. Several recent actions could affect U.S. alien immigration policies, including the Aristide letter abrogating the 1981 treaty and the new State Department policy providing for U.S. detention of all illegal migrants. From your experience as commander of the Haitian Migration Task Force, what impact do you think these actions are likely to have on the Coast Guard's migrant interdiction efforts?

Answer. If the bilateral agreement is abrogated it would increase the time required to repatriate Haitian Migrants. Haiti is the only country with which we have a bilateral migrant nterdiction agreement. Without this agreement, we would continue to repatriate migrants, but would rely on ad hoc arrangements with Haiti to repatriate migrants, just like we currently do with most other oUfltries. This would result in operational delays while awaiting he outcome of diplomatic negotiations. The State Department advises that they do not have a new policy for U.S. detention of all illegal immigrants and that such an immigration policy would come under the purview of the Department of Justice (Immigration and Naturalization Service).

However, if a mass migration were to occur, with thousands of Haitians immigrating to the United States at once, abrogation of the 1981 treaty would greatly impact our ability to control migration. In a mass migration, most all of the Coast Guard's Atlantic cutter and aircraft fleet would be involved in interdicting migrants and rescuing those in unseaworthy craft. To handle repatriation of thousands of migrants on an ad hoc basis would be enormously difficult.

CERTIFICATES OF FINANCIAL RESPONSIBILITY

Question. What is the status of the Coast Guard's rulemaking regarding certificates of financial responsibility under the Oil Pollution Act of 1990?

Answer. Department policy precludes me from discussing the status and direction a final resolution of this matter might take. I can assure you that the Coast Guard is considering all comments very carefully, takes the concerns raised by shipowners and operators seriously, and has no intention of taking any action that would cause severe economic disruption.

DRUG INTERDICTION

Question. I understand that one of the Commandant's new responsibilities will be to serve as the U.S. Interdiction Coordinator for Federal drug-enforcement activities. What are the requirements of this position, and how do you view the Coast Guard's role in drug interdiction?

Answer. The U.S. Interdiction Coordinator (USIC) will act on behalf of and be responsible to the President of the United States and the Director, Office of National Drug Control Policy (ONDCP) for interdiction efforts of the United States consistent with the objectives of the National Drug Control Strategy. The USIC will oversee coordination in the Western Hemisphere, up to, but not including the borders of the United States (as defined by interagency agreement). This tasking includes non-operational and non-tactical oversight coordination of all aspects of detection and monitoring, sorting, and apprehension supported by U.S. resources.

The USIC will coordinate the efforts of departments, and agencies with overseas interdiction responsibilities, ambassadors, and senior military commanders/civilian managers to:

—Ensure that assets committed by departments and agencies to international interdiction are adequate.

—Integrate the location and scheduling and optimize the employment of U.S. aerial and maritime detection/monitoring and interdiction assets.

The USIC will be advised by a committee of concerned Agencies and shall refer unresolved issues to the Director, ONDCP for decision.

With regard to the Coast Guard's role in drug interdiction, the U.S. Coast Guard, as the nation's primary maritime law enforcement agency, has responsibility for the enforcement of U.S. laws in the maritime arena, the lead agency role for maritime drug interdiction and co-lead with U.S. Customs for airborne drug interdiction. Consequently, our maritime transit zone interdiction responsibilities remain intact as an essential element of the National Drug Control Strategy.

We continue to conduct interdiction missions, with emphasis upon interagency counterdrug cooperation and efficiency. In addition, with the assistance of the State Department, we are pursuing international counterdrug cooperative efforts and host nation institution-building initiatives. The Coast Guard also participates in a variety of interagency efforts designed to improve the efficiency of U.S. Government counterdrug efforts.

FOSTERING DEVELOPMENT OF MEASURES, STANDARDS, AND PRACTICES

Question. You have stated your intent to "foster development of international measures, standards, and practices, in both commercial vessel safety and marine environmental protection." What do you mean by this statement, and how would you achieve it?

Answer. We intend to lead the development of a comprehensive set of internationally recognized standards for use by the maritime industry.

There will be an active participation through leadership roles in international standard making organizations such as International Standards Organization and International Electrotechnical Commission in addition to International Maritime Organization. We also intend to promote the development of international standards compatible with U.S. standards and industry practices.

Our next endeavor will be the development of a comprehensive set of nationally recognized, internationally compatible set of standards for use by the U.S. maritime industry. There will be active participation through leadership roles in national standard organizations such as American Society of Mechanical Engineers, American Society of Testing and Material, and Natioanl Fire Protection Association, and the promotional development of internationally compatible and competitive national shipbuilding standards.

We will also strive to improve competitiveness of the U.S. maritime industry by removing regulatory and other barriers that impede productivity and free flow of commerce and replace detailed regulations with internationally and nationally agreed standards. We will also promote performance based standards rather than detailed specifications as the means of compliance.

Finally, we will increase the Coast Guard knowledge base through cooperative endeavors and exchanges of information with industry.

QUESTIONS ASKED BY SENATOR HOLLINGS AND ANSWERS THERETO BY ADMIRAL HENN

Question. Admiral, if confirmed as Vice Commandant, what role do you expect to play in the day-to-day management of the Coast Guard?

Answer. Admiral Kramek and I have, of course, discussed this at some length. Due to the complexity of the issues involved, I expect to work very closely with the Commandant. sharing the responsibility and the work associated with that position, both in the establishment of policy and management of day-to-day functions of the Coast Guard, expect to be the Commandant's closest advisor in all matters relating to the Coast Guard as well as Chair the Senior Advisory Group which consists of all three star Admirals.

Additionally, I plan to work with the representatives of the Chief of Naval Operations board as Co-Chair of the NAVGARD board. I intend to discuss and resolve the use of Coast Guard and Navy resources to increased mutual benefit.

DOWNSIZING THE COAST GUARD

Question. The Coast Guard currently numbers 88,000 personnel, including active duty, auxiliarists, reservists, and civilians. What do you see as the biggest personnel challenges now tracing the Coast Guard with respect to downsizing the Federal Government and maintaining current mission requirements? If confirmed, how do you propose to address these challenges?

Answer. Our greatest challenge as we re-engineer and streamline the Coast Guard in support of the President's and the Secretary's goals is to preserve the core infrastructure necessary to ensure the delivery of essential Coast Guard services to the public and to fully support the organization remaining. Preserving properly maintained multi-mission assets and a quality, well trained, well motivated, fullysupported workforce is critical to the success of the Coast Guard's downsizing efforts.

We will continue to refine our multi-year budget strategy adopted for fiscal year 1995. This multi-year approach examined all Coast Guard programs for potential savings and efficiencies. The primary consideration in this review was preservation of the Coast Guard's unique blend of core capabilities, characteristics and attributes * * * and its ability to execute core missions and responsibilities by providing essential services to the public. In reviewing the Service's mix 6f operational and support resources, certain critical characteristics and capabilities were given priority:

—Maintaining a multi-mission capability with a sound command and control structure;

—Ensuring sufficient, well maintained operating and support facilities;

—Preserving the military nature of the service and its unique combination of capabilities that provide the President flexibility to respond to ongoing and evolving national security scenarios, to carry out national policy, and to respond to domestic crises;

—Preserving the unique mix of Coast Guard's law enforcement authority and capabilities;

—Preserving the capabilities to ensure safe transportation on the nation's waterways;

—Preserving essential elements of the support infrastructure so as to maintain an adequate readiness and response posture; and

—Maintaining a well trained, motivated and professional workforce.

Two major studies are underway to explore opportunities for economies and efficiencies. The largest of the two will review the command and control and support infrastructures. The second study will review all aspects of Coast Guard training programs and resources. Numerous smaller initiatives are also underway to study the possibility of savings in other aspects of our overhead. All of these initiatives are seeking possible areas for savings which streamline processes, removes layers and seek to empower employees. I must emphasize, however, that inspite of these efforts, we won't identify true efficiencies or economies in every case.

People remain our greatest asset. At the same time we are seeking ways to streamline the Service, we are working hard to minimize the stress of transition for those employees leaving the Coast Guard and to improve the working environment for our employees that remain. Incentives will be used to encourage employees to voluntarily leave and a central clearinghouse of job vacancies will be established to facilitate the transfer of employees from targeted areas. Training will be provided if specific job specialties are reduced and a corresponding vacancy is not available.

Question. For 21 of the 31 years you have served in the Coast Guard, you have worked in the field of marine safety and environmental protection. Given this background, what are you priorities for improving commercial vessel safety, and what domestic and international steps would you take to deal effectively with the environmental and safety threats posed by substandard commercial vessels?

Answer. My primary goal is to substantially reduce deaths. injuries and economic loss associated with commercial vessel accidents. I have set the following specific performance goals to achieve this objective during my term:

- Reduce deaths and injuries from maritime casualties by 20 percent.
- Prevent any passenger vessel casualty with major loss of life.
- Improve the safety of commercial fishing from its "most hazardous" ranking to at least halfway toward the median of all industrial occupations.
- Remove any competitive disadvantage from Coast Guard regulatory and compliance programs, with no degradation of safety.
- Eliminate substandard commercial vessels from U.S. waters.

Domestically, we are eliminating substandard ships from U.S. waters implementing the targeting regime described in the Coast Guard's Report to Congress of April 8, 1994. Implementation includes:

- Establishing foreign ship boarding priorities based on ship's flag, class society, owner, age, and history.
- Ensuring performance records of owners, class societies, and flag states are determinant factors in setting boarding priorities.
- Increasing the frequency of boardings on those ships most likely to be found in a substandard condition.
- Assigning marine inspectors to foreign freight ship boarding teams to increase expertise and scope of boardings.
- Aligning Coast Guard efforts with international initiatives by relying on two-tiered boarding process with greatest effort and most detailed exams reserved for substandard ships.

Internationally, we are eliminating substandard ships by aggressively supporting IMO measures to ensure other Flag States fulfill their responsibilities. International measures include:

- 11Establishing an international casualty data base.
- Development of guidance for port state control inspections and surveyor training.
- Development of model agreements between administrations and organizations acting on their behalf.
- Development of standards for organizations acting on behalf of administrations.

RECREATIONAL BOATING SAFETY

Question. In recent weeks, we have heard from recreational boaters on a number of issues, including license fees for marine radios, termination of boat safety grants, and legislative proposals to require that young children wear life jackets. How will these issues affect recreational boating safety and what would you suggest to improve the Coast Guard's relationship with the boating public?

Answer. We have some concern that the proposed Federal communications Commission license fee for marine (ship) station licenses will discourage owners of vessels not required to carry radios, primarily recreational vessels, from carrying essential safety equipment, such as VHF marine radios, emergency position indicating radiobeacons (EPIRBS), and radar. This equipment, although not required on recreational vessels, greatly enhances safety and significantly improves the Coast Guard's ability to provide assistance in emergencies.

Because funds appropriated from the Boat Safety Account of the Aquatic Resources Trust Fund for the State Recreational Boating Safety (RBS) Grant Program are scored no differently than Coast Guard operating expenses, the State RBS Grant Program, of necessity, had to be considered a potential candidate for reduction to meet mandated budget targets, in competition with other Coast Guard programs. In the context of significant operational and personnel resource reductions, and the adverse impact of additional operational resource cuts which would be necessary if the Coast Guard were to continue the State Recreational Boating Safety Grant Program, the administration concluded that the grant program should be offered as part of the agency's budget reduction package. This preserves the Coast Guard's ability to continue essential services to the recreational boating public, as well as the maritime industry as a whole. While the administration budget proposes to terminate the discretionary appropriation for the State RBS Grant Program, the States will continue to receive Federal boat safety funds under the mandatory appropriation transferred from the Sport Fish Restoration Account of the Aquatic Resources Trust Fund to the Secretary of Transportation, as provided by the Clean Vessel Act of 1992, which increases from $7.5 million in fiscal year 1995, to $10 million in 1996 and 1997, and $20 million in fiscal year 1998.

The National Recreational Boating Safety (RBS) Program was established to promote greater State participation and uniformity in boating safety efforts, to encourage the States to assume a greater share of boating safety education, assistance and enforcement activities, and to enhance the safety of recreational boating. Today, the States have assumed major responsibility for boating safety, collectively spending over four times the amount of funding provided by the Federal Government for State boating safety grants. The States are the Coast Guard's closest partners in efforts to ensure the safety of the millions of American boaters, and we will continue to cooperate with and support State efforts.

The Coast Guard concurred with the provision of the Recreational Boating Safety Improvement Act of 1994 (H.R. 3786) which would require that each individual 12 years of age or younger wears a Coast Guard approved personal flotation device when on an open deck of a vessel under 26 feet in length. Wearing life jackets is the most important boating safety intervention practice, and while the number of children who die in boating accidents is relatively small, those losses are no less tragic. We are hopeful that children will carry the habit of wearing personal flotation devices forward as they continue boating throughout their lives, and thus have a significant positive long term impact on boating safety.

Recreational boaters are the Coast Guard's largest constituency, and they are very important to us. The Coast Guard will continue to provide essential services to recreational boaters and try to ascertain and be responsive to their needs to the greatest degree possible. The cooperative National Recreational Boating Safety Program has been very successful. The boating fatality rate is only one-fifth of what it was when the Federal Boat Safety Act was enacted in 1971. We will strive to continue to improve this noteworthy record.

The boating public can be assured the Coast Guard remains c-ommitted to improving boating safety within federal funding constraints. It is important to note that the Coast Guard will continue to oversee the national boating safety program, and provide key boating safety services, including maintaining our full support for Coast Guard Auxiliary activities, boating education programs and safety information pamphlets, boating safety compliance testing and boat recall campaigns, establishing or updating boating safety rules and regulations, as well as maintaining our essential multi-mission stations and Aids to Navigation facilities to ensure an adequate emergency Search and Rescue capability and safe U.S waterways. We will also continue to coordinate safety enforcement activities with he states and provide grant funds for boating safety activities of national non-profit service organizations.

Senator INOUYE. And may I now call upon the Vice Commandant-designate, Adm. Arthur Henn. Admiral Henn.

STATEMENT OF REAR ADM. ARTHUR E. HENN, VICE COMMANDANT-DESIGNATE, U.S. COAST GUARD

Admiral HENN. Good morning, sir. I am honored by my nomination to the position of Vice Commandant of the U.S. Coast Guard, and I too am pleased to appear before you and this distinguished committee today.

As Chief of the Office of Marine Safety, Security, and Environmental Protection, I have worked closely with Admiral Kramek in his capacity as Chief of Staff of the U.S. Coast Guard. We have shared work on many initiatives and projects. I believe that my vision for the Coast Guard mirrors that of Admiral Kramek, who is a good friend and a superb boss. For the next 4 years, I both enthusiastically and wholeheartedly support his vision and his direction.

My Coast Guard responsibilities during the last 31 years have given me hands-on experience in areas of personnel management, strategic planning, budgeting, management information systems, emergency response, and international negotiation. I have enjoyed a range of operational and support assignments. During this latter part of my career, I have spent most of my time in maritime safety and marine protection-type assignments. I look forward to the support that I can give to Admiral Kramek in these priority areas of the Coast Guard.

Admiral Kramek and I have complementary career paths that will give our management team the ability to lead the Coast Guard in a strong and coordinated direction. I am committed to preserving the Coast Guard's multimission flexibility and its national security capabilities. I am truly excited about the contributions that we can make to the national transportation system and look forward to expanding our partnership within the Department of Transportation.

I am very pleased to have this opportunity to serve as Vice Commandant of the world's premier maritime service. I pledge that I will focus my energies in support of the administration, in support of this Congress, and in support of the next Commandant.

Sir, together we will effectively and efficiently manage the Coast Guard and provide the quality services that the American public so rightly deserve.

Thank you, sir.

Senator INOUYE. Thank you very much, Admiral Henn. I am certain you have noticed that only three of us are present here, but I would like to assure you that the absence of members does not in any way indicate the lack of interest.

At this moment, it may interest you to know there are 11 committees and subcommittees meeting at the same time, and on these 11 committees our colleagues are now serving as members, so we cannot be at two places at the same time, but we three have several things in common. The three of us are senior members of the Appropriations Committee. We three are senior members of this committee. We three represent coastal States. We consider the Coast Guard very important to us, so anything you want you get. [Laughter.]

The CHAIRMAN. Senator Inouye is right on target. We are somewhat hamstrung.

Let me just ask one question, and we are going to ask Admiral Kime to appear.

If we are closing under the request for 1995, 14 of the 166 multimission boat stations, we decommission 11 of the 195 multimission cutters, we lay up 9 of the 180 multimission aircraft, and then put you in as the coordinator, the U.S. coordinator of interdiction, drug interdiction, how do you cut back all of these things and then really do the job that is a growing task rather than a diminishing mission, or am I wrong? Are we somehow changing from interdiction to something else?

I know this must bother you coming in. Are you happy about this? Do you like these cuts?

Admiral KRAMEK Well, no, sir, I certainly do not like the cuts, but I think cuts were imposed on us last year as a budget reduction. I believe it started in the House to do that, anticipating that there would be a reduction in the administration's drug interdiction program and anticipating there would be a major change in policy.

There has been a major change in policy—some of it is classified, but the policy in the interdiction program is one of operations in the transit zone and chasing people while they are on the way here—to more emphasis in-country and to stop the cocaine, as an example, at its source, so I think some of those reductions in our budget last year that caused us to have to lay up these assets were made without seeing what the whole policy was going to be.

We cannot do the whole job that we were able to do last year, this year, and certainly there are less assets now employed in the war on drugs in the deep Caribbean. Since December 15, 1993, perhaps only 60 or 70 percent of the assets are employed in the interdiction mode now that were employed prior to the budget cuts.

The CHAIRMAN. Well, I guess it is really, then, a problem for this individual Senator in that this trying to get the drugs at its source—I visited recently one of the major sources; namely, Bolivia, and in the old expression at home it is whistling Dixie.

I mean, you have got a vast country there. Its livelihood is growing cocaine. Its cultural habit is chewing it. Just get into the city of La Paz, up 14,000 feet high, and see 1 million men and women walking the streets chewing the stuff.

You look at its policy, and they have got an off-limits area, so to speak, of where it is grown bigger than the State of Georgia. It has also got a policy if they planted it before 1988, they can continue to plant it, and stopping it at the source is defined as the little processing entities, little plants around here there and yonder that move like the old liquor stills did in my back yard during the Prohibition days, and it is next to impossible. It is just not working. I do not know where we got that change in policy. We need to start interdiction right here on 14th Street in the District, and we ought—not the Coast Guard, obviously, but I mean, all interdiction, and you right at the coastal areas is the best we can do.

Admiral KRAMEK I would like to respond to that a little if I may, Senator, that when I was the interdiction coordinator for the drug czar in the Caribbean and the Southeast portion of the United States, the job was a little bit similar, but not on a national level like I will have now.

There is no one solution, as we all know, to stopping the war on drugs. It is a balanced program, a balance between the many elements of the supply side, interdiction being one of them, and many elements on the demand side.

A new national strategy has been put together, and my role as interdiction coordinator will be to make sure that the various agencies who have responsibility under that strategy are allocating the resources they have to do the job, and that it is being wisely done, and that they are asking for sufficient funds in their budget to implement those various portions of the strategy, and then to make sure they are coming up with measures to show that in fact they are doing that.

The in-country situation in Bolivia, along with interdiction in the transit zone, along with demand programs and education programs in the United States, and perhaps a dozen other things in the national strategy, we will attempt to bring into the best balance we can for the money that is available to do the best job we can. Without a credible interdiction program, I think the demand program does not have credibility with the public, so we will do the best we can with the resources we have, sir.

The CHAIRMAN. Well, that is it. Both you and I are disturbed about the credibility of it.

Senator Stevens.

Senator STEVENS. Thank you very much.

Admiral, I noted as we prepared for this hearing that roughly $200 million, or 5 percent of the Coast Guard's budget, is spent on equipment and facilities in Alaska each year, and that you have a total now of 2,069 people, personnel stationed in Alaska.

We do not have 5 percent of the population of the country, obviously, but we have got one-half the coastline in the United States. Alaska is the last great area of the United States that has superb fishing—the U.N. study shows that ours is the top of the list. Alaska has the first and the second largest fish landing ports in the United States. I think we have the largest in the world, really, now, at Dutch Harbor. At least nine countries trying to fish our 200-mile zone in the North Pacific.

The Coast Guard has been given the authority to enforce the U.N. ban on driftnets, and our own national ban on driftnets. You have the authority to enforce the international agreement that closes the so-called donut hole. You enforce the ban on catching salmon more than 45 miles from any nation's shoreline. You have a series of duties under the Marine Mammal Act and other acts that are designed to protect the marine mammals of our area.

I am fearful, however, that as I see this budget come down, that there is sort of a population ratio to expenditures of the Coast Guard. Do you see what I see in terms of a bare minimum staffing, as far as the Alaska duties are concerned?

I think you are stretched very thin. There are no Coast Guard helicopters west of Kodiak. The largest fishing fleet in the world is out there with no Coast Guard helicopter capability for search and rescue—except on a very long flight out of Kodiak. I understand in the summertime you do put one at Cold Bay once in a while.

I am worried that the pressures of the budget are going to reduce the service that I think Alaskans rely on more than any other Americans. Have you had a chance to study our situation in Alaska and the North Pacific in general?

Admiral KRAMEK Yes, sir, I have, and I can report to you that at least for this current year—I believe the Commandant will testify to that at the follow-on hearing that this committee will have this morning—that we do not have any major plans at all to reduce our assets or activity in Alaska.

As you said, 66,000 miles of shoreline, an Exclusive Economic Zone that goes out 200 miles from there is just an enormous area, and you forgot to mention—and I am sure you did not, sir. You live up there and have lived your life there—what the weather situation is and the windows of opportunity and how dangerous it is especially for fishermen coming out of Dutch Harbor.

Senator STEVENS. My son, who is a captain of a fishing vessel out of Dutch Harbor, reported to me that on two occasions he went out with two other boats and his came back alone. When you realize those odds, they are staggering.

Admiral KRAMEK Some of the most dramatic search-and-rescue cases I have been involved in in my career as captain of a ship in the Bering Sea were rescuing fishermen from Dutch Harbor on the way up toward the fishing grounds by St. Paul.

It is dangerous. We are fully employed in Alaska. We put our major assets there and recently moved around two 378-foot cutters. In fact, we are relocating a couple more aircraft in Kodiak, helicopters that we are reducing from other places in the United States, in order that we can have more helos to equip our ships for the missions that you suggested. We are fully employed with all our assets and are not looking to reduce any. We cannot. We have too much business there.

The CHAIRMAN. If the Senator would yield, what is the danger, fog or turbulent seas there, or what?

Senator STEVENS. It is the combination of wind and sea conditions.

Admiral KRAMEK It is wind and sea conditions. About every 12 hours another front comes through. They are very violent, very sharp. It is very dangerous. A mariner in that area has to bide his time and look for a window of opportunity when he can do anything, and that applies to the fishermen as well.

Senator STEVENS. And add to that the load of ice that comes along with changing conditions.

Admiral KRAMEK And 32-degree water temperature.

Senator STEVENS. Thank you very much. Well, I am pleased to hear that. I really do worry about the status of the Coast Guard in Alaska. The distances are so great.

Last summer, I know that four driftnet vessels were intercepted there in the North Pacific, fishing contrary to the ban. One had to be escorted all the way back to Shanghai. That took one of your vessels away for 3 or 4 weeks. It is really a hard duty area for the Coast Guard, and I would hate to see it reduced. If anything, I would like to see some improvements. But we will go into that later with Admiral Kime.

The CHAIRMAN. Senator Inouye.

Senator INOUYE. Thank you very much, Mr. Chairman. I would just like to make a statement. Of all the agencies of our Government, the least understood and the least appreciated in my mind is the U.S. Coast Guard.

Because Coast Guard personnel, our men and women, put on a uniform that looks military in nature, I believe most Americans look upon the Coast Guard as part of the military structure of the United States, and accordingly, when the military drawdown was made part of the policy of the United States the Coast Guard was caught in the web.

Actually, at this time, if anything the Coast Guard funding should be increased. Certainly the strategic nuclear threat of the Soviets has diminished, and one can justify a military drawdown. However, it did not mean that the threat of drugs have diminished. I think the chairman has pointed that out. Just as many, if not more fishermen now sail the seas, and they need to be assisted.

We hear about your activities in the coast of Bosnia, and the Persian Gulf, the Indian Ocean, and the Caribbean, but I think most Americans should be made aware that your activities go far beyond that, and I would hope that my colleagues in the U.S. Congress will take note of your full comprehensive mission.

Somehow I think we have failed to advise the people of the United States of the importance of the Coast Guard, that you are in the Mississippi River, you are off the shores of South Carolina, you are helping the fishermen in Alaska, you are helping our yachtsmen in Honolulu—your work extends all over the world.

I do not think it should be part of the military drawdown, and Mr. Chairman, I am going to do my best to point out this strange dilemma that the Coast Guard is in at this time, because what we are doing is we are hurting ourselves.

The CHAIRMAN. Well, I join fully in the observations made by my distinguished colleague from Hawaii, and would add on to that that they were throwing down the bridges as we were trying to cross the Rhine in December 1944, and we got run back for a while.

I was with the Coast Guard at Fu Bac in Vietnam, down in what we call the I Corps area, and when we increased the size of the United States under the Magnuson Act by one-third, the responsibility thereby was a sort of police force; namely the Coast Guard to take over that one-third addition to our jurisdictional responsibility, and then come back each time, cutting it, cutting it, but you are right, we all thought it was the military.

I came to a Commerce hearing 27 years ago and saw a few of the Admirals outside and said, you are mistaken, the Armed Services is two floors down in the Dirksen Building, and I sat up and we had the regular hearing, and I could see Senator Magnuson said, now, we have got some hearings here to confirm the nominations of the Coast Guard. Where are they? Where are they? I had sent them down to the Armed Services. [Laughter.]

So, you are right. I am the one that made that mistake, but I have tried to recover from that, and giving full support always to our Coast Guard, because I have served on the board up at the Academy and I have seen them go out in the middle of the night, go up on the side of a vessel 30-feet high, just three guys with a rifle in their hands, just throwing a rope, and take over a tanker full of marijuana 100 miles off the coast of South Carolina and bring it in. They have got all kinds of courage and are tremendously dedicated, but undersupported financially if nothing else.

Senator Mathews.

Senator MATHEWS. Thank you, Mr. Chairman. As I think the panel knows, being from Tennessee our coastline is very short, so my concerns and my questions and my interests, Admiral, I guess may better be addressed to the next panel, but it relates to the boating safety program that is referred to in the testimony I think that will be given here later this morning.

Our State, those of you who can visualize the geography and layout of the State, it is a little over 100 miles wide and perhaps 110 miles wide, and it is almost 600 miles long. We have six Interstate highways traversing the State, but our lake coastline, our internal coastline, is 5 miles longer than the Interstate Highway System in our State, so the boating safety program which funds are collected from fuel taxes and have been disbursed to the States through the Coast Guard, is of very significant importance to us.

I have read the information in the testimony, and I have read the special letter by Admiral Kime with respect to this. I want to submit for the record here for whichever panel should consider this a letter from one of our wildlife resources agency members, and a resolution by that body addressing this question, and ask, Mr. Chairman, if I could, if at an appropriate time we could get a response to that.

I understand that sometimes we in the Congress, in the way that we set up programs, almost force a type of action that came here, because you had the choice of either reducing this program and knowing the funds were going to find a way to the State anyway for another purpose, though, but knowing that the funds were going to find a way, or reducing your own program.

Probably if I had been in your shoes I would have done exactly the same thing you did, but nevertheless, the way that the program is structured, the States are going to be losing valuable funds which were raised for that purpose, and—in the end they will not lose them, but they will given to them for a different purpose than what they would have been used for under this.

I would simply ask that if there are some suggestions that you have, or your personnel have, that would help us in restructuring or doing it better, that you give us the benefit of those thoughts.

Thank you, Mr. Chairman.

The CHAIRMAN. Very good. We have some additional questions for the record from our distinguished colleague, Senator Breaux, and our distinguished House Member over on the House side, Congressman Rose, and we will submit those questions for the record.

We appreciate the appearances of both of you here this morning.

[Whereupon, at 10:35 a.m., the committee adjourned.]

○

APEX
TP_CF
9780160468551